DISCLAIMER

Copyright © 2025 by Alison Dunlop
First published in 2025. All rights reserved.
Published by Storyline House Publishing
www.storylinehouse.com

No part of this book may be reproduced, stored in, or transmitted in any form or by any means – electronic, mechanical, photocopying, recording, or otherwise – without prior written permission from the publisher, except for brief quotations (under 10%) used in reviews, articles, or for other non-commercial purposes as permitted under copyright law.

The information in this book is provided for general purposes only and does not constitute professional, financial, medical, or legal advice. Readers are encouraged to use their own judgment and seek appropriate guidance based on their individual circumstances.

While every effort has been made to ensure accuracy, neither the author nor the publisher accepts any responsibility for errors, omissions, or any loss or consequences arising from the use of this material. The author and publisher disclaim any liability for any direct or indirect damages resulting from the application of the information contained herein.

Every individual is unique, and results may vary. Please adapt the ideas and insights in this book to suit your own needs and situation. By reading and using this book, you acknowledge and accept full responsibility for your choices and outcomes.

Publisher: Storyline House Publishing
Publishing Support and Production Oversight: Sarah Jayd
Author: Alison Dunlop
ISBN: 978-1-7638270-2-8
For distribution or rights inquiries: hello@storylinehouse.com

About Storyline House Publishing: *An independent publishing house dedicated to supporting writers and authors on their self-publishing journey. We believe every storyteller deserves the tools, guidance, and confidence to bring their book to life. From concept to completion, we provide high-touch support, creative direction, and professional expertise, empowering authors to publish independently while retaining full ownership of their work.*

Our mission is simple: *To make self-publishing easier, more accessible, and deeply rewarding – so every story finds its voice and every author leaves a legacy.*

www.storylinehouse.com

PREFACE

A Welcome to Your Unfolding

"May you shine YOUR Light in ways only you can."

Hey beautiful soul,
This book isn't a how-to or a spiritual checklist.
It's more like a soul companion. A moment to exhale. A permission slip.
You're allowed to outgrow who you used to be.
You're allowed to feel a little lost while something deeper is finding its way to the surface.
You're allowed to heal in ways that don't look tidy.

Inside these pages you'll find a mix of stories, soul wisdom, insights from the healing room, and those little phrases I say all the time without realising they're medicine. (You'll see what I mean.)

Before you start reading, let's set a gentle intention – to honour your journey.

Place your hand on your heart.
Take a gentle breath, and affirm:
"I give myself permission to be exactly where I am. I honour my journey and welcome what is true for me in this moment."
And so we step forward with love and wonderment.

Alison x

Author's Note: Read this book with a highlighter in hand. Underline the bits that resonate, the words that feel like they were written just for you. Those are the breadcrumbs you'll want to return to later – your own soul notes tucked in the margins.

ABOUT THE AUTHOR

Alison Dunlop

Alison Dunlop is an intuitive kinesiologist, energy healing practitioner, writer, and soul guide based in regional Queensland. For over 12 years, she has helped her clients release emotional baggage, shift limiting beliefs, and reclaim their spark after years of giving to everyone but themselves. Working both in-person and online, Alison has guided hundreds of clients back to authenticity, balance, and inner connection.

Her work is a fusion of science and soul. In her healing room, she blends advanced kinesiology with vibrational essences, oracle guidance, and channelled insight – creating a space where sensitivity is honoured, truth is uncovered, and healing unfolds with gentleness and power.

Known for her voice that is both nurturing and real, Alison meets people where they are, offering reflections and practices that spark subtle yet profound transformation.

Her debut book, *'Becoming You'*, carries the heart of her work onto the page. Inspired by sacred client stories and her own lived experience, it offers one powerful reminder: you are not broken – you are becoming.

Through her sessions, courses, and writing, Alison continues to help women feel more grounded, more connected, and more at home in their own skin – reminding every reader of the light they have always carried within.

- https://alisondunlopkinesiology.com.au/
- https://www.facebook.com/alisondunlopkinesiology
- https://www.instagram.com/alisondunlopkinesiology/
- https://www.linkedin.com/in/alison-dunlop/

A Soul Invocation
by Alison Dunlop

Rain seeps through the cracks
Tender caress from above
A gentle guiding hand weaves
Shimmers of galactic poetry abides
Wisdom tendrils with passion
Signs are afoot
A space of quiet adornment

I am becoming

AUTHOR'S NOTE:

This poem arrived as a spontaneous soul whisper – channelled in quiet presence, before I even knew where it belonged.

Now I see… it was always meant to begin here.

These words are an invitation for you to soften, to listen, and to allow your own unfolding.

Welcome home, beautiful soul.

INTRODUCTION

The Soul Spark

I didn't set out to write a book. Truthfully, I never really thought I would. When it was first suggested to me, I said to myself, *"No way!"* It felt too big. Too exposing. Too… much.

But then something shifted. I knew I had to do this. And once I said yes – it flowed.

I believe I've been guided here, to offer what I've seen, what I've lived, and what I know in my heart. Not because I have it all figured out. But because I've walked this path – the one where you forget your own light because you're just trying to function. Just trying to keep up.

This book isn't here to fix you. It's here to remind you – again and again, of your true essence. Your light. Your soul.

Remember: You are unfolding – perfectly, in your own time and at your own pace.

Over the past 12+ years as a holistic practitioner, kinesiologist, and energy worker, I've sat with hundreds of clients, listening, witnessing, holding space for their pain, their growth, their becoming.

This book was born from those sacred moments. It's a soul companion – something to gently whisper to the parts of you that feel tired, unsure, or forgotten. Something to help reignite what's always been within you.

Inside, you'll find personal reflections, healing room moments, simple energy teachings, and the phrases I say all the time without even realising they're healing gems. (I call them Alisonisms.)

You'll also find some affirmations and gentle practices – not to overwhelm, but to support. To anchor you in your own wisdom. Because this is the Soul Spark.

This journey isn't about striving. It's about trusting.
It's about uncovering what you already know.
And remember - always.
You are allowed to gently evolve here.
You are allowed to rest.
You are allowed to come home to your own light.

CONTENTS

Chapter 1: The Soul Beginning 3

Chapter 2: You're Not Broken – You're Becoming 11

Chapter 3: Trusting the Unseen 19

Chapter 4: Essence Over Identity 29

Chapter 5: The Reclamation of the Heart 41

Chapter 6: The Architect of Soul 51

Chapter 7: Sacred Stillness and Soothing 65

Chapter 8: Becoming You – Stepping Into What's Next 79

Chapter 9: Poetry in Motion 91

Closing Words: A Love Note to the Becoming One 99

A Bonus Chapter: "Becoming One – Alisonisms
from the Healing Room" 101

CHAPTER ONE

The Soul Beginning
(The moment of inner awakening.)

I believe we're all born with a soul. It's our essence – the real part of us that lives beyond roles, expectations, or even this lifetime. It stays with us, life after life, gently guiding us home to ourselves.

The soul isn't something outside of you. It's energy. It lives in the body. It speaks through your feelings, your instincts, your reactions, and those moments when something just feels true – even if you can't explain why.

In my clinic, I see the soul emerge in all kinds of ways. Through the body. Through emotions. Through beliefs. Even through the words someone says without realising. People often come in saying they're tired, stuck, or off-balance. But underneath that? The soul is stirring.

The soul is always guiding us back into alignment. Back to ourselves.

And it's not always loud. Sometimes it's just a spark. A pull. A gut feeling. A knowing that doesn't come from the mind. And sometimes, when your soul is conflicted, when something you're doing doesn't sit right, or a value or belief feels off, you feel it as an ache. A heaviness. A quiet discomfort that's hard to name, but impossible to ignore.

So where is the soul?

I believe it lives in the heart space. That's where we often feel its ache, its warmth, or its longing. But it moves throughout the body too. The third eye – that spot between your eyebrows – is like a little periscope to the soul. It helps us tune into the deeper truths, especially when it's open and clear.

But the soul isn't only in one place. It's in your chest when it tightens. It's in the tears that show up out of nowhere. It's in that deep sigh when something finally feels aligned.

And no matter how long it's been, your soul is still there. Waiting. Ready.

We're often looking outside ourselves for answers – especially when it comes to our life purpose. We chase roles, goals, or expectations, trying to be what we think we should be. But in the process, we miss our soul's quiet call completely.

It doesn't have to be complicated. Sometimes, it starts with a sacred pause. A moment of stillness. Just being. That's often all it takes to begin reconnecting with who you truly are underneath it all.

But here's the thing: most of us forget. We don't always know that we're soul-led beings. We don't know what we don't know.

From the moment we're born, we pick up stories about who we should be. We learn what to do to be loved, accepted, or safe. Some of those stories aren't even ours.

They come from:

- **Family patterns and ancestry** – passed down through generations. Things like *"don't cry"*, *"keep going no matter what"*, or *"we don't talk about our feelings"*. You might be carrying the emotional weight of people you've never even met, simply because that's how your family coped with hard things.

- **Past life imprints** – sometimes, people carry fears or patterns that don't make sense in this lifetime. Like being terrified of speaking up or having an unexplained sense of guilt or grief. These can be echoes from other lives where things went wrong. I've actually witnessed people in clinic release vows of silence, fear of persecution, or beliefs tied to being punished for having power.

- **Childhood experiences** – what you were praised or punished for, what you had to do to feel safe or seen. If you learned early on that love came when you were quiet, perfect, or helpful, it shapes how you show up now.
- **Society's pressure to fit in** – we're taught to be busy, productive, and successful. Rest gets labelled as lazy. Sensitivity gets labelled as weak. We're told to have it all together – and if we don't, we feel like we're failing.
- **Gender and status roles** – women have carried the weight of being unseen or powerless for centuries. Our worth used to be tied to our husband's name or our ability to serve others. Men have been told to "man up", that being sensitive isn't strong, and that their value is in what they provide. These beliefs can run deep – through bloodlines, culture, and unspoken rules.

Some patterns go even deeper – linked to trauma, fear, and survival. I've worked with clients who carry the imprint of being hurt, silenced, or controlled in generations past. These are not just memories, they're energetic signatures we hold in the body until we're ready to release them.

I explain to clients sometimes our patterns and imprints are like a messed-up ball of wool that the cat has played with. It's a tangle of old threads that can block us from hearing our own truth. But it can be cleared. It can be gently untangled and released.

In clinic, in fact, that's what I help people do. We work through those layers. We gently lift the old beliefs, patterns, and pressure that don't belong. And when that happens, they feel something shift.

The soul's voice gets louder. More honest. Clearer.

You begin to hear your own inner voice again. Not the noisy one shaped by fear or habit, but the quiet one underneath, the one that's always been there.

Sometimes that voice sounds like a whisper. Sometimes it comes through your body. And sometimes it arrives as a gentle nudge from something greater.

Soul Synchronicities: The Universe Leaves Clues

Sometimes the soul doesn't speak in words – it speaks in winks. Little whispers from the universe that land at just the right time, nudging us back onto the path. We call them synchronicities.

They might look like repeating numbers on the clock – 11:11, 2:22, 4:44 – or hearing a song lyric that feels like it was written just for you. They might show up as meeting the right person at exactly the moment you needed them, or noticing the same phrase or idea pop up in three different places in a single week. Sometimes it's as simple as a feather on your path, a butterfly circling you, or a book falling off the shelf when you were seeking clarity.

In my clinic, I've noticed repeatedly how the music playing in the background seems exactly what the client needs to hear. A lyric will land at the very moment a client shares something vulnerable, and we both know it's not random. It's a cheeky universal nudge that spirit weaves through lyrics into our healing journey.

These moments are not coincidences. They're reminders. Gentle whispers that you are guided, that you are not alone, that your soul knows the way.

And how do you know when it's a true synchronicity? Often your body tells you. Goosebumps ripple down your arms. A yawn escapes as energy shifts. Tears rise unexpectedly. Or there's simply a knowing – a deep, quiet recognition that this was meant for you.

When you notice these signs, pause. Breathe them in. Smile at the mystery. Because each one is a sacred nod from the universe saying, *"Keep going, beautiful soul. You're on the path."*

I therefore believe we are never truly alone on this path. I have felt the presence of my guides many times – in moments of uncertainty, always in clinic, and even the car. In quiet moments, there is a soft knowing that seems to come from beyond me. Angels have walked beside me too. Sometimes I call on them with intention, but most times I simply feel them arrive.

When I ask for help, I often turn to *Archangel Michael* to clear fear or confusion, or to help me release energy that doesn't belong. I feel his strength like a shield. And when I need comfort, I call in *Mother Mary*. Her energy is soft but steady, like being wrapped in a warm shawl, or light.

Everyone connects differently. Some feel a sense of their ancestors. Others receive symbols or synchronicities. You might not know who or what you're connecting with at first – but your soul does. And your spiritual team is always listening.

This chapter, this book, this journey – it's about remembering that part of you.

Because you are not broken. You are not behind. You're becoming. And your soul already knows the way.

A Sacred Pause – Begin Here:

Take a moment. Place your hand gently on your heart. Close your eyes if that feels safe.

Breathe gently. In and out. Feel the warmth of your hand radiating through your chest. Let yourself soften into it.

This is you connecting with your soul. Not striving. Not fixing. Just being.

Alisonism

"You don't know what you don't know."

And that's okay. How often do we beat ourselves up for past actions, when honestly, we didn't have the knowledge or strength to change our situation at the time? So, forgive yourself for not knowing what you didn't know, and cut yourself some slack.

"All soul journeys begin – in the not-knowing."

Questions to Ponder and Journal

When have I felt a whisper or nudge from my soul – even if I didn't recognise it at the time?

_____

_____

_____

_____

_____

What signs or synchronicities seem to show up for me again and again?

_____

_____

_____

_____

_____

If I pause and place my hand on my heart, what truth is waiting quietly beneath the surface?

_____

_____

_____

_____

_____

CHAPTER TWO

You're Not Broken – You're Becoming

(Honouring that 'in-between' healing space.)

The soul itself is whole, wise, and eternal. But through human experience – trauma, grief, shame, abandonment – we can feel disconnected from our soul. That disconnection can feel like brokenness.

And that feeling? It's real. It deserves to be seen and held with compassion.

In my clinic, I've seen this over and over. People come in saying things like:

"I just don't feel like myself anymore."

"I'm fine on the outside, but I feel empty inside."

"I should be happy, but I'm not."

"I feel stuck."

"I don't seem to be able to move forward."

"I don't know my direction."

These are soul signals. Signs that something deeper is stirring – asking to be heard, acknowledged, and gently healed.

When we've experienced deep hurt, especially over time, parts of us pull back. The soul doesn't break, but it can go into hiding. It's like a light dimming to protect itself.

This can happen slowly. Bit by bit, we stop listening to ourselves. We ignore that intuitive gut feeling. We quiet our needs. We shrink, we people-please, we adapt, and we don't even realise we've drifted away from our essence.

In energy healing, this might be described as soul fragmentation. Little pieces of your energy that have scattered due to overwhelm or pain. The more scattered you feel, the harder it is to connect to your centre or your soul space.

This can sometimes feel like you are a genie in a bottle. The essence is still there – powerful, magical, full of potential – but sealed inside. Contained.

Life's hurts, expectations, and beliefs become the bottle. You're still in there, but everything feels compressed. Limited. Pressurised.

The good news is even the tightest bottle can't hold back a soul forever.

When the cork begins to loosen, even just a fraction, something shifts. A crack of light slips in. The air feels different, less stale. You might not burst free all at once, because most of us don't, but there's a sense of breath returning, of possibility.

For some, it arrives as a sigh, a sense of relief they didn't know they were holding. For others, a release of tightness or pressure, with a sense of lightness. Sometimes it's just the smallest flicker of hope, a reminder that the genie has always been magical, even when pressed against the glass.

This is the moment the soul begins to stretch again. To remember its size. To reclaim its sparkle. Not broken. Not lost. Just waiting for space to shine.

For me, there were moments in my past where I lived in that heavy, pressurised space. Not broken but suspended, sometimes barely functioning. I couldn't fix the ache or put things back together because it was out of my control. All I could do was just keep going the best

I could and hoped the Universe could hear my prayers and come through with some guidance. Amongst the tears, I always had faith in my spiritual team, even when things were hopeless and didn't make sense. That faith kept me hanging on. It reminded me that I would be guided to a better space, and that I wasn't totally alone.

But here's the truth: The soul doesn't shrink, and mine certainly didn't. It waits, in protective mode. And when the seal starts to lift – when safety returns and space opens, the soul begins to stretch again. It expands, breathes, and radiates.

That's what soul healing can feel like. Not always dramatic or instant. Sometimes it's a soft unfolding. A gentle return.

You might start feeling more like yourself. You start to laugh again. You remember what brings you joy. You stop hiding – not because you've fixed everything, but because you're reconnecting with what's always been within you.

That is not coincidence. That is healing. That is becoming.

It can feel uncomfortable, and messy, but this is where the magic begins.

Let's take a breath together. Let's honour the part of you that showed up here, even while still mending. Because this? This is where the becoming begins.

A Gentle Practice: Offering Safety to Your Inner Child

Take a quiet moment. Place one hand on your heart, the other on your belly. Breathe gently for a few moments. Let your shoulders soften.

Now, imagine your younger self standing beside you. It might be the child who felt unseen, scared, or unsure. It might be the version of you who first learned to shrink or hide.

You don't need to fix her. Just hold her hand. Let her know:

"You didn't do anything wrong. You were doing the best you could. I see you. I love you. You're safe now."

If it feels right, say gently:

"I forgive you for not knowing what you didn't know."

"I forgive you for being so hard on yourself."

"I forgive you for the times you neglected your own needs just to get through."

Now just be with her. No rushing. No agenda. Just presence. Just be in the feeling. Ask her softly:

"What do you need right now?"

Listen. Don't force. Just notice.

Spend a little more time with her if it feels right.

Now gently, give your inner child a hug. And as you do – give yourself a hug. Cross your arms around your body. Lean into it. Let the warmth of that embrace be felt.

Let your breath deepen. Let your body receive the safety of this moment.

This is the soul re-weaving. This is becoming.

Acknowledgement and permission is the start. Just naming where you are and giving yourself space to feel it – that's a powerful beginning. You don't need to have it all figured out. You just need to say:

"I'm here. I'm listening. I'm willing."

This chapter is about honouring that part of your journey – the in-between space. The space where you don't feel like the old you, but you're not sure who you're becoming yet.

And if you're still in the in-between? That's okay too. You don't need to transform overnight. You're allowed to be a work in progress. Give yourself permission to take it one step at a time. Let that truth take the pressure off. You don't have to force change or rush your becoming. The soul unfolds in its own time – not according to anyone's expectations, including your own.

A Sacred Pause: Let the Angels Hold What You Can't

You can ask *Archangel Michael* to help you release what no longer serves, as he's the protector – the one who cuts energetic cords and clears emotional debris with powerful, loving precision.

And if what you need most is to feel safe, comforted, and deeply nurtured, call in *Mother Mary*. Her energy wraps around you like a soft blue light or blanket – tender, reassuring, full of grace.

When you find yourself struggling to express what's inside – when the words won't come, or when you're afraid of being misunderstood – invite *Archangel Gabriel* to stand beside you. Gabriel is the messenger, the bringer of clarity. His energy clears foggy thoughts, softens fear around speaking, and helps your truth find its way into words.

And for the times when your heart feels heavy or your body is weary, call on *Archangel Raphael*, the healer. Raphael's green light flows like a balm, soothing emotional wounds and reminding you that you are held in divine wholeness. He restores hope, strengthens your spirit, and helps you remember that healing is always possible, even if it comes one breath at a time.

Let them in. Let them hold the parts of you that are too tired to keep going.

A Gentle Angelic Release Practice

Find stillness. Sit or lie down. Let your exhale be longer than your inhale. Soften.

Place your hands over your heart. Whisper:

"I give myself permission to let go, even if just for now."

Call in Archangel Michael.

Visualise his deep cobalt blue light clearing the weight from your body.

"Michael, help me release what no longer serves. Restore me to my truth."

Invite Mother Mary to come close.

Feel her gentle presence as a beautiful blue rose blooming in your chest, or like a warm shawl gently wrapped around your shoulders.

"You are safe to rest now."

Now welcome Archangel Gabriel.

See his light as pure white or golden, washing over your throat and mind.

Feel your thoughts clear, your words soften, and your truth rise gently to the surface.

"Gabriel, bring clarity to my mind and courage to my voice. Help me express what is true."

Finally, call upon Archangel Raphael.

Sense his emerald green light flowing through your heart, lungs, and body like a healing balm.

Let it soothe any aches, release heaviness, and restore hope.

"Raphael, heal what feels tender. Restore my heart and spirit to wholeness."

Close with this affirmation:

"I am supported. I am loved. I am free. I am becoming."

Alisonism

"Please forgive me for not loving you the way you needed. I didn't know how, but I am with you now."

Questions to Ponder and Journal

What would it feel like to offer myself gentle compassion, rather than pressure?

_____

_____

_____

_____

_____

What message might my inner child want me to hear right now?

_____

_____

_____

_____

_____

CHAPTER THREE

Trusting the Unseen
(Learning to release the grip and follow soul guidance.)

Trusting the unseen can feel like a stretch – especially when life feels messy or uncertain. We want the map. The guarantees. The 'right' choice laid out before we take the next step.

But the soul doesn't work that way.

In clinic, I often describe it like this:

You're in the car. You've typed your destination into the Navman. And now... you have to trust it'll get you there. You don't throw the Navman across the seat because it's not showing you every single street at once. You follow one turn at a time.

We want the whole map, every street, every outcome. But that's not how the soul works. Even in the car, you don't see the entire journey laid out in one glance – you see one section of road at a time. And that's enough. If you had the whole map, you'd probably get overwhelmed, second-guess every turn, or forget to look out the window and enjoy the ride.

Your soul – your intuitive guidance system – works the same way.

It speaks quietly. It nudges. It doesn't lay out the full journey in bold print – but it knows the way. The trouble is, we often grip the steering wheel of life so tightly that we miss the turnoff our soul is trying to guide us toward.

We want control. We want certainty. But what we really need is trust.

Sometimes the most powerful thing we can do is let go of the grip... and set cruise control. Not because we're giving up, but because we're choosing to surrender to a bigger guidance system.

Sometimes the bigger guidance can also be a whisper from our spirit team – an angelic nudge, a soul guide adjusting the route when we feel lost. You might not realise it, but those quiet urges, those out-of-the-blue ideas or changes in direction – they can come from beyond your conscious mind. From guides, ancestors, angels – the unseen energetic support team that travels with you.

This chapter is your permission slip to release what's weighing you down. To soften your shoulders. To stop gripping so hard. And to believe that you are being led – even when the road isn't clear yet.

Sometimes, it's not just the steering wheel we're gripping – it's the whole load we're carrying.

Picture this: You're on a soul road trip... but the boot is overflowing. Past regrets. Old beliefs. Generational expectations. The pressure to be perfect. You've overpacked for a journey that was always meant to be lighter.

No wonder the car isn't performing.

It's clunky. Heavy. Stalling on the hills.

At some point, you've got to pull over, open the boot, and ask: *"Do I really need this?"*

Some of it was never yours to carry. Some of it served a purpose once, but it's not aligned with where you're heading now.

You don't need to unpack it all at once. But you can choose to release what's no longer helping you move forward.

This is the part of the journey where you lighten the load. You trust that who you are becoming doesn't need to carry everything you once did. You give yourself permission to travel differently now.

A Soul Practice: Unpacking the Boot

Take a moment. Close your eyes if that feels safe. Breathe gently and imagine yourself beside your soul car – parked safely on the side of the road.

Now picture yourself opening the boot.

It's full. Old beliefs, fears, responsibilities, expectations, shoulds, and even ancestral and societal burdens… Some of them are dusty. Heavy. Taped up with other people's names on them.

One by one, start to take them out. As you hold each item, ask:

"Is this mine to carry?"

"Is this still serving me?"

"Do I want to bring this into the next part of my journey?"

If the answer is no, place it by the roadside. Thank it. Bless it. And let it go. Place yourself in your own protective energetic bubble.

Feel the weight lift. Feel the air shift. Notice what it feels like to travel lighter.

Maybe there's space now for joy. For peace. For the unexpected.

And while we're here, it's worth asking: *"What kind of car are you travelling in?"*

Is it shiny and well cared for – polished, vacuumed, full of fuel, with the service up to date? That's what it feels like when you're looking after your energy, tending to your body, and clearing out what doesn't belong.

Or is it running on fumes, cluttered with old coffee cups and lolly wrappers, with the 'service due' light blinking at you every time you turn the ignition? That's the version of us that's giving to everyone else, ignoring our own needs, and pushing through even when we know it's time to stop.

Neither one makes you a bad traveller. They're simply clues. Just like your actual car, your soul vehicle needs maintenance. It needs fuel that nourishes you, regular check-ins, and the occasional deep clean. When you honour that, the journey becomes smoother – not because life is perfect, but because you've prepared your vehicle to carry you with more ease.

Alisonism

"Your soul car runs best when you actually stop to fill the tank."

When you're ready, close the boot. Slide back into your seat. And whisper to yourself: *"I'm allowed to release what no longer serves me."*

Trusting Without the Full Picture

Here's something I see often – in clinic, in friends, in myself: We wait.

We wait until we're confident. Until we're certain. Until we have all the answers. Until the fear disappears.

But soul work doesn't work like that.

Sometimes, the next step only appears after you take the first one. This was certainly the case for me as I worked through each chapter of this book.

Imagine you are walking through fog. You can't see the whole road. You might only see a few steps ahead – but that's enough. That's how trust works.

Trust says: *"I don't know exactly where this is going... but I'm willing to follow what feels right."*

And that willingness? That's where the magic begins.

You don't need a five-year plan. You don't need to wait for perfect clarity. You just need to be present enough to feel your next yes.

The soul doesn't demand certainty. It asks gently for your hand.

The Signs Along the Way

As you travel, it helps to remember: You're not driving alone. The universe is riding with you – sending signs, nudges, and soul messages all the time.

Be on the lookout for synchronicities. Pay attention to what shows up around you.

What's playing on the radio? A song, a sentence, a lyric you didn't expect – and yet it lands like it was just for you and gives you soul chills.

Sometimes it's a bumper sticker with a phrase that lands right when you need it. Other times it's a licence plate number that repeats the same sequence you've been seeing everywhere. Or it might be a billboard, a street name, or a bird swooping past the windscreen at the exact moment you were thinking of someone you love.

In my clinic, I've often noticed how the music playing at the exact moment a client shares something carries the answer they've been searching for, and it can bring tears or laughter. The same happens on the road, the lyrics that come through the radio can be a direct message for your soul journey.

How are you feeling in the car of your life?

Do you need to wind down the window and let something go? Are you craving warmth – a moment of care, comfort, kindness? Turn on the heater or wrap *Mother Mary's* shawl around you.

Can you see clearly through the windscreen? If things are foggy, maybe it's time to pause. Switch on the demister. Let the mist clear gently, instead of pushing through blindly.

Open the sunroof. Let the light in. Do you need to feel the freedom of wind in your hair?

This journey isn't just about getting to your destination. It's about being aware. Being present enough to notice what the divine is whispering to you as you go.

Even though you may not have a clear destination yet. That's okay, because soul journeys aren't always about knowing exactly where you're going. Sometimes it's about taking the next step… or the next leg of the trip.

Maybe you just drive for now. One turn at a time. One breath at a time.

And don't forget the sacred rest stops. The places where you pause, stretch, take in the view. Those soul pauses aren't wasted time – they're where integration happens.

Remember also, when you notice you're carrying something heavy – a belief, a pressure, a story, or even a conflict – pause and ask yourself, *"Is this mine?"*

Occasionally, especially if you are a sensitive, you may pick up on other's baggage without even realising. It's like having a stowaway in the boot of baggage.

After you have asked is this mine, and realised it's not, it's best to let this baggage go, because it's not yours to keep. Bless it and send it back to the universe with love. Say to yourself: *"I am 100% myself."*

Continue on your journey feeling lighter and clearer.

And while travelling along – don't forget to maintain your vehicle.

Check in with your tyres. Are they balanced? Inflated? Or are you running yourself flat?

How's your battery? Are you recharging regularly – or running on fumes?

What kind of fuel are you giving yourself? Are you surviving on the bare minimum, or are you choosing the premium kind – nourishing food, soul connection, spiritual rest, emotional renewal?

Looking after your body and energy isn't a luxury. It's sacred maintenance. It keeps you on the road.

When the Road Isn't Moving

Sometimes, no matter how much you trust, no matter how prepared you are – the road stops.

There's a traffic jam. An unexpected detour. An emotional breakdown or life event that throws your timing right out the window.

And suddenly, you're not sure what to do. Do you wait it out? Take the next exit? Or just sit there and breathe through the frustration?

Here's what I've learned – sometimes the pause is the path.

Delays don't always mean you're off track. They often mean: Not just yet. Wait. Something's still settling, or something is coming.

In clinic, I see this all the time – people feel stuck and assume they've taken a wrong turn. But often, they're just being asked to pause. To listen and to trust.

Sometimes, it's being in the midst of a traffic jam that the most powerful insight arrives.

Other times, yes – it's time to take a new road. But it's not about rushing ahead. It's about tuning in.

Ask yourself: *"Am I pausing because I'm avoiding something? Or... am I being asked to stay still so I can receive something important?"*

Both are valid. Both require trust.

When You Reach a Fork in the Road

And then there are times when the road splits – and you have to choose.

Both paths might look fine. Neither one feels wrong. But your soul is whispering… and it's asking you to listen.

This is the fork in the road.

It's not always about making the perfect decision – it's about making a conscious one. Tuning in. Heart connecting and asking, *"Which path feels more like freedom? More like truth? Or more right?"*

Sometimes the answer is clear. Sometimes you just choose – and trust that whichever road you take, you'll grow.

One path may feel heavy, tight in the chest, like you're dragging your feet. The other may feel lighter, freer, even if it's unfamiliar. That's how the soul speaks – not through logic, but through sensation.

You don't need to analyse it. Just ask yourself:

"Which path feels more like freedom? Which feels more like truth?"

And trust the answer that comes, even if it doesn't make sense yet.

Even the 'wrong' turn can lead to the right becoming.

So you're never truly off course. You're just gathering what your soul came here to learn.

Alisonism

"There is never really a wrong turn, it's a learning."

Soul Travel Check-In

Before you take your next step, ask:
"Am I gripping the steering wheel too tightly?"
"Do I need a rest stop – even a short one?"
"Is this belief mine to carry, or can I release it with love?"
"What's the next gentle step I can take – even without the full map?"

Mantra for the Road

"I trust the timing. I trust the signs. I am safe travelling the road of life."

CHAPTER FOUR

Essence Over Identity

*(Letting go of roles and labels to return
to the essence of your soul.)*

We wear so many hats.

Mother. Taxi driver. Partner. Provider. Caregiver. Business owner. Friend. Fixer. Listener. The one who holds it all together.

Some roles are obvious. Others go unnoticed or undervalued.

The role of caregiver – whether to a child, partner, parent, or client – is one of the most sacred, yet often the most under strain. It asks so much of us and rarely gives us the chance to refill our own cup.

Some roles we step into with pride. Others we inherit.

And some we outgrow without even realising it – until they begin to feel tight, heavy, or misaligned.

In clinic, I often work with people who feel like they've lost themselves. Not in one big moment – but over time. They've layered on so many identities to keep others comfortable, to survive, or to be seen as 'enough'.

Often, they're operating in constant overwhelm – barely functioning, tending to others, and holding everything together without ever truly stopping to ask, *"What do I need?"*

But underneath it all… they feel so distant from who they truly are.

That's where kinesiology is powerful. It helps to gently peel back the layers – like an onion.

Each session brings awareness. A belief. A feeling. A role under stress.

We start to see what was once invisible. And that's where healing gradually begins.

I know for me, Kinesiology sessions were my saviour at a time when anxiousness took over my barely functioning overwhelmed body.

Sometimes the stress sits in a particular role – like mother, business owner, or partner.

The body tells us what the mind has been trying to push through.

Tightness in the chest. Fatigue. Anxiety. Agitation. Feeling like you're always 'on'.

These are nervous system clues that a part of you is calling to be witnessed.

And it's not just this lifetime.

I've worked with clients where the stress runs deep in the family line.

A great-grandfather who had to suppress his sensitivity.

A man hardened by war, who was never allowed to cry.

That energy gets passed down.

It might show up as a father who can't show affection, or a woman who feels she must always be strong, and unable to show tenderness.

We carry these layers – and sometimes, they're not even ours!

Some great examples from clinic include instances where some of my female clients who still to this day reject their femininity and confidence, because of the roles their ancestors played in lifetimes gone by.

We also carry beliefs about how we're meant to look.

Body image, cultural programming, and societal norms affect so many of us, even subconsciously.

The body as identity.

I've seen dysmorphia, shame, and self-comparison tear many of my women clients away from their essence – all because they've absorbed an idea of what's 'acceptable' or 'beautiful'.

Yet the soul truth is completely different.

And then there's imposter syndrome.

I know that one well.

As a practitioner and business owner, I've compared myself to others.

Questioned if I'm doing it right.

Wondered if I'm enough, because the business model says otherwise.

It's wild – because I know I'm amazing and passionate about what I do.

But when you don't fit the 'standard model', it's easy to doubt yourself.

I've learned that I don't need to run my business like anyone else.

I'm not cookie cutter.

I'm intuitive.

I let my soul essence lead – not the numbers, the noise, or what anyone else is doing.

That's what this chapter is about:

Letting go of the performance. The pressure. The patterns that dim your light.

And perhaps most importantly – being gentle with yourself along the way.

You're allowed to be a work in progress. You're allowed to take your time.

Essence doesn't rush. It unfolds.

And when we release the pressure to 'have it all together', we give ourselves the grace to actually become.

You are not your roles.
You are not your body.
You are not your business structure.
You are essence.
And essence doesn't need to prove itself.
It just needs permission to be felt.
To be trusted.
To be lived.

Remembering Your Soul Essence

So how do we even know what our soul essence is?

It's not something you figure out in your head.

It's something you feel!

It's the part of you that existed before the world told you who to be.

Your essence is often revealed in moments of quiet…

When no one's asking anything of you.

When you're not performing or proving.

When your shoulders drop and your heart softens.

Sometimes, your soul essence shows up when you least expect it.

For me, it happened one Sunday – lying on the couch, just chilling.

And then… poetry started flowing.

Words literally just fell into my consciousness.

Ancient words I didn't even know the meaning of – words I needed to interpret.

Not from my mind – but from something deeper. My knowing. My essence.

This book is the same.

I didn't start with a plan. I had no outline. No 'how-to'.

But as I've written, it has unfolded – chapter by chapter, truth by truth.

That's essence.

When you trust what wants to come through you, instead of trying to control it.

A Sacred Practice: Entering the Heart Room

Find a quiet space.

Let your body soften. Let your breath slow.

Pause for a few moments. Breathe gently. Just be.

Gently place your hand on your heart.

Close your eyes if that feels right.

This is your invitation to be with yourself. Nothing to fix. Nothing to perform. Just be.

Now, with your awareness, imagine stepping inside your heart.

See it as a room – your heart room.

This is your personal heart room. It does not need to look a specific way. Go wild with your intuition!

So what does yours look like?

Is it light? Dark? Spacious? Cozy?

Are there colours? Is there furniture?

Take a slow walk through this space.

Notice any colours, shapes, sounds, or symbols.

Maybe there's something waiting for you here – an angel, a spirit, your inner child, an object, a memory, a message, or a feeling.

Whatever there is here for you, know you are guided and safe here.

Ask gently:

"What does my heart want me to know?"

"Is there a message here for me?"

Please be gentle with yourself and trust whatever appears, and whatever messages you receive. This is a space where your heart and soul speaks.

If it feels right you can also ask gently:

"What part of me is ready to be seen again?"

"What truth have I been holding inside?"

You don't need to analyse. Just feel.

Lean into whatever arises.

When you're ready, thank your heart.

Let the image soften.

Take three deep breaths and gently ground yourself with your breathing.

And remember: you can return to this room anytime.

It belongs to you.

*

Author's Note: For a long time, my heart space literally consisted of a huge red welcoming red lounge with cushions, which I would throw myself on to, and give myself five minutes to breathe. This space was the only space I could feel any peace or sense of me. My heart space became my sanctuary, even if for a few minutes, to start the healing process.

Some clients also tell me their heart room experience takes them to the beach – a place of salt air, waves, and where they can feel some fleeting freedom. Others have found themselves walking quietly through a forest, surrounded by tall trees and soft light. Whatever arises is deeply personal, and often exactly what the soul needs at that moment. And your heart room may shift and change too – what feels right one day may look completely different the next.

A Gentle Exercise: Updating Your ID Badge

We spend much of our lives wearing metaphorical ID badges – labels we've absorbed or taken on to navigate the world.

They might say:

Mother, Boss, Good girl. Strong one, Hard worker, Peacemaker. Always fine.

Some we chose.

Some were handed to us.

And some have stayed far longer than they should have.

These badges aren't who we are. They're who we've been expected to be.

What a realisation!

This is your invitation to pause – and check in.

Take a moment. Visualise yourself holding your current ID badge.

What roles, labels, or expectations are written on it?

Now ask yourself:

"Do these still fit? Is this badge still valid or has it expired?"

"Do they reflect who I truly am, or just who I've had to be?"

If you're feeling ready, imagine setting that badge down or throwing it in the bin.

Feel the freedom!

It's now time to create a new one!

What might your updated ID badge say?

Becoming. True. Sacred. Creative. Unbound. Free to be me. Work in progress.

There is no pressure here – just go with whatever resonates with your essence in this moment.

There's no rush. Just permission to feel.

To honour who you are now – and who you're becoming.

A Soul Practice: The Mirror of Essence

Find a quiet space and stand before a mirror. Take a slow breath and soften your gaze. You're not here to critique or judge – you're here to meet yourself.

Place a hand gently on your heart. Let yourself see you – not the roles you play, not the masks you've worn, but the soul that shines through your eyes.

Whisper to yourself:

"I give myself permission to be me."
"I honour who I am becoming."
"My soul essence is enough."

Stay here for a moment. Notice if emotions stir, or if you feel a sense of tenderness rising. Allow it. This is your soul's reflection – the part of you that has always been present, beneath every identity.

When you're ready, smile softly at your own reflection. Close with a hand-to-heart breath, anchoring the feeling of permission and presence into your body.

Alisonism

"My past does not dictate my future."

Give yourself permission to turn the page and start a new chapter in your story book..

Questions to Ponder and Journal

Which identities or roles do I cling to most tightly?

_____
_____
_____
_____
_____

How do I feel when I imagine myself without those roles?

_____
_____
_____
_____
_____

What qualities or feelings arise when I connect with my true essence or Soul?

_____

_____

_____

_____

_____

Where in my life can I give myself more permission to simply be me?

_____

_____

_____

_____

_____

CHAPTER FIVE

The Reclamation of the Heart
(Soul-led heart healing, and forgiveness.)

Becoming you starts with gentle heart healing.
Before the clarity. Before the confidence.
Before the soul whispers grow loud – the heart has to feel safe enough to open again.
When there's no love for self – for whatever reason – the soul dims.
Not because it disappears, but because it retreats.
The soul is light, and that light needs a safe place to land.
And that place… is your heart.
The heart and soul are deeply connected.
When the heart is closed – from pain, shame, disappointment, or emotional exhaustion – the soul becomes harder to hear.
It doesn't stop speaking. It just softens into the background.
And we begin to forget that we are lovable, worthy, and enough.
In clinic, I've seen this so often.
Clients come in holding so much – stories, roles, grief, pressure.
Sometimes they can name the moment their heart closed.

Other times, it's just a heaviness they've carried for years, or even lifetimes. A tiredness in the chest. A sense that love is something they've always had to earn.

Often, this links back to the inner child.

The little one who had to be strong, quiet, or perfect just to feel safe.

The one who kept everyone else happy, but never learned how to care for their own heart.

And now, the adult is still operating on those same settings – giving, proving, coping – without feeling truly loved.

This could even be ancestral patterning, where the soul didn't feel safe.

Now this is where reclamation begins.

Not by pushing the heart open.

But by gently creating space for it to unfold, like a butterfly.

To breathe again. To feel safe enough to soften.

The Heart's Wisdom

The **HeartMath Institute** teaches that the heart is more than just an organ – it's intelligent.

It communicates with the brain. It holds emotional memory.

It sends out an electromagnetic field that can be measured several feet outside the body.

The heart isn't just a physical organ – it's an intelligent energy centre. Science shows that the heart generates the body's most powerful electromagnetic field. In fact, researchers at the HeartMath Institute have measured that the heart's electromagnetic field can extend two to three metres beyond the body.

That means your heart is not only influencing your own nervous system, emotions, and brain – it's also interacting with the people around you. You've probably felt it before: walking into a room and sensing whether it feels calm and welcoming, or tense and uncomfortable. That's your heart field picking up information, long before words are spoken.

When we shift into heart coherence – when our thoughts, emotions, and breath align – our field becomes more harmonious. Not only do we feel calmer inside, but others around us often respond differently, too. It's a reminder that reclaiming our heart isn't selfish – it's a gift that ripples outward.

When we focus our attention and breath into the heart space, we create coherence – a state where our heart rhythm becomes smooth, steady, and calm.

Heart coherence is more than just a nice feeling.

It's measurable. And it's powerful.

HeartMath studies show that coherence can:
- Lower cortisol (the stress hormone)
- Improve clarity and decision-making
- Reduce anxiety and emotional overwhelm
- Strengthen the immune system

- Support deeper sleep and resilience

But one of the most beautiful discoveries?

When you're in a state of coherence, the field around you shifts – and it influences the people and animals nearby. This is truly incredible.

Real Life Heart Connection

I've seen this in clinic so many times.

A client walks in scattered, anxious, or shut down.

Before we even start the balance, I place my hand on my heart, take a few soft breaths, and drop into coherence myself, without even realising it.

And then… there is a shift.

I start to calm, and so do my clients.

Their breathing noticeably slows.

Their shoulders drop.

And they say something like, *"I feel better just being here."*

That's not magic. That's the nervous system responding to energetic safety.

When we're settled, others feel it – even without words.

It's why babies calm on their mother's chest.

Why friends feel lighter after sitting in a safe space.

Even animals pick up on this – they sense the shift, and it helps them settle too.

One of my favourite HeartMath experiments involved a boy named Josh and his dog, Mabel.

They were each fitted with heart monitors. When Josh entered the room and focused on loving feelings toward Mabel, their heart rhythms synced – without any physical touch or talking.

It was pure, heart-felt connection.

When we are in a state of calm love, it changes the energetic field around us – and this is amazing.

This is love you can feel.

And it's a reminder: you don't have to force love to return.

You just need to create the space for it.

A Soul Practice: Heart Coherence Breathing

Step 1: Find stillness

Place your hand on your heart.

Let your breath slow down.

You don't need to fix anything. Just be here in gentleness.

Step 2: Slow your breath

Inhale gently for a count of 5…

Exhale softly for a count of 5…

Let the breath be smooth and steady.

Step 3: Breathe through your heart

Imagine the breath flowing in and out of your heart space.

Let each inhale bring calm… each exhale release tension.

Step 4: Bring in a warm feeling

Think of someone, something, or somewhere that brings you comfort or gratitude.

It could be a memory, a pet, a place in nature, or a quiet moment of joy.

Feel it in your heart.

Step 5: Let it settle

Stay here for a few more breaths.

Let your body and nervous system soak in this feeling.

This is heart coherence.

The Forgiveness That Frees the Heart

As your heart begins to soften, another layer may begin to rise – forgiveness.

Not the kind you force.

Not the kind that says, *"Just let it go."*

The deep, honest kind – the kind that lifts weight off your chest.

Sometimes, it's about forgiving yourself.

For past choices.

For how you coped when you didn't know better.

For giving too much, or staying too long, or forgetting your own needs.

Sometimes it's forgiving yourself for not knowing how – how to speak up, how to set boundaries, how to receive love without guilt.

And sometimes, it's forgiving yourself for being treated badly – and blaming yourself for it.

We also carry stories that don't belong to us.

Ancestral wounds. Family burdens.

You are allowed to forgive what was never yours to hold.

You are allowed to stop punishing yourself for things that weren't your fault.

This kind of forgiveness doesn't erase the past.

But it creates room.

Room for the heart to breathe.

A Gentle Forgiveness Practice

Place your hand on your heart.
Take a soft, steady breath.
Speak to yourself like someone you love, or to your inner child.
"[Your Name], I forgive myself for..."
Let whatever needs to rise come through gently.
It might be:
"... not knowing what I didn't know."
"... being treated badly and thinking it was my fault."
"... believing I had to keep giving just to be loved."
Now say:
"I release this burden. I don't need to carry it anymore. I choose to move forward with love."
Breathe.
Lean gently into these words.
Let them meet you where you are.
This is a moment of freeing yourself.

Alisonism

"Forgive me for not knowing what I didn't know."

Questions to Ponder and Journal

When have I noticed my heart closing – and what helped it feel safe to soften again?

_____

_____

_____

_____

_____

What stories, roles, or burdens have I been carrying in my heart that are no longer mine to hold?

_____

_____

_____

_____

_____

Who or what do I need to forgive – not to excuse the past, but to free my own heart?

_____

_____

_____

_____

_____

What does heart coherence feel like in my body? How can I invite more of that into my daily life?

_____

_____

_____

_____

_____

If I truly believed my heart was a safe sanctuary, how might I live differently?

_____

_____

_____

_____

_____

Alison's Mantra for the Heart

"I am one. I am love."

CHAPTER SIX

The Architect of Soul
(Taking ownership of your inner life.)

There comes a moment when you realise... you're not just healing from your past – you're building something new.

This chapter is about that turning point.

When you shift from surviving to consciously designing.

From default to soul-led creation.

This is the exciting bit – you become the architect of your soul.

An architect doesn't build randomly.

They take time to honour the foundations.

They draw up plans.

They consider both structure and beauty.

They build for longevity – not just appearances.

You can do the same.

You don't need to know every detail – but you can start shaping what you want your inner world to look and feel like.

The soul holds a blueprint – a design for your life that already exists within you. You don't need to see the whole plan to begin. Architects don't stand still waiting for the entire building to reveal itself. They begin by laying foundations.

It's the same with your soul. Every choice, every habit, every thought is like selecting your building materials. Are you choosing bricks of truth, compassion, and trust? Or flimsy scaffolding built from old patterns, self-doubt, and 'shoulds'?

The strength of your inner world comes down to your foundation. Without it, even the most beautiful designs can collapse under pressure. With it, you can weather storms and still stand strong.

Just as an architect spends time planning, sketching, and preparing before building begins, your soul is asking you to pause and honour your foundation. What values will hold you steady? What practices will support you when life tests your walls?

Because being the architect of your soul isn't about rushing to the finish line – it's about creating something that will last.

The Soul Company

In clinic, I often share this idea:

You are the CEO of your inner world.

You're not just a passenger in your life.

You're running something powerful – your energy, your beliefs, your values, your emotional space.

Let's call it your Soul Company.

And like any good company, yours needs a few key foundations:

• **A code of ethics** – these are your soul values.

The non-negotiables that guide how you live, lead, and love.

Maybe it's honesty, compassion, creative freedom, or rest without guilt.

• **Policies and procedures** – not boring paperwork, but the way you choose to run your life.

How you make decisions when you're tired.

How you respond when someone crosses a boundary.

How you protect your energy after a full day of giving.

How you return to centre when things feel messy or chaotic.

• **Regular maintenance and training** – because healing and growth don't stop when the session ends.

This might look like checking in with yourself weekly, learning new ways to respond to stress, saying yes to support, or upgrading outdated patterns.

Sometimes it's knowing when to book in with a kinesiologist, a trusted practitioner, a psychologist, or a doctor – someone who can support the maintenance of your emotional, energetic, or physical well-being.

• **Clear boundaries** – because not everything gets full access to your time, energy, or nervous system.

Boundaries might look like logging off at a certain time, protecting your creative space, or saying no to emotional baggage that isn't yours.

Sometimes, it means drawing the line – clearly and kindly – and holding it, even when it's uncomfortable.

- **The courage to hire and fire** – beliefs, habits, roles, or ways of thinking that either align with your soul... or don't.

You might fire the overachiever who keeps you running on empty.

You might rehire Joy, who's been waiting at the door.

You get to restructure any time.

And most importantly... you need a contract with yourself.

Not a rigid agreement – a sacred one.

Something that says:

I choose to honour myself.

I commit to leading from alignment.

I give myself permission to adjust, refine, and return to what feels true.

And remember:

Even the most successful Soul Company has quiet support staff you don't always see.

Your spiritual team, your angels, the universe itself – they're in the background, holding you, whispering guidance, nudging you toward alignment.

You are never doing this alone.

Alisonism

"When my soul leads, everything else falls into place."

∾

Your Inner Team

Every company has a team – and so do you.

Inside your Soul Company, you have different parts of you showing up each day.

Some are helpful. Some are overworked. Some are ready to retire.

You might recognise a few:

- **The People Pleaser** – trying to keep everyone else happy (this was me)
- **The Inner Critic** – never satisfied
- **The Fearful Protector** – keeping you small to stay safe
- **The Overachiever** – proving your worth through doing
- **The Resilient One** – strong, but tired
- **The Creative** – full of ideas, waiting for permission
- **The Inner Child** – needing love, reassurance, and play
- **The Wise One** – intuitive, calm, and steady

You get to meet these parts.

Acknowledge them.

And decide who stays, who gets a new role, and who's ready to be gently let go.

The Soul Company Blueprint

You're the architect.
Let's lay the foundations.

Step 1: Meet Your Current Team
Write down the inner parts of you that show up often.

_____
_____
_____
_____
_____

What roles are they playing? Are they helping or holding you back?

_____
_____
_____
_____
_____

Step 2: Review the Roles
Who's in alignment with who you're becoming?

_____
_____
_____

Who's running outdated scripts?

Who needs rest, support, or a new job title?

Who can you lovingly thank... and release?

Step 3: Rewrite the Structure

What values does your soul company run on now?

_____
_____
_____
_____

What's your mission or focus at this stage of life?

_____
_____
_____
_____

What kind of support do you need to bring in next?

_____
_____
_____
_____

Even small changes shift the whole system.

A Soul Practice: The Foundation Stone

Every lasting structure begins with a foundation stone – the solid base that supports everything else.

Close your eyes and imagine standing before the blueprint of your soul company. In your hands, you're holding a stone – smooth, weighty, grounding. This stone will become the cornerstone of your inner foundation.

Ask yourself: *"What word do I want etched into this stone? What quality will hold me steady no matter what?"*

It might be love, trust, compassion, freedom, courage, or another word that rises from deep within you. There's no wrong answer – just what feels true for this moment.

See yourself carving that word into the stone. Feel its weight. Feel the strength it gives you.

Now, in your mind's eye, place the stone at the base of your soul structure. Know that every choice, every practice, every step forward will rise from this foundation.

When life feels shaky, you can return to this stone. Rest your hands on your heart and whisper your word. Let it remind you that you are building something strong, lasting, and true.

A Soul Contract with Yourself

Place your hand on your heart.
Take a soft breath.
Then say:
"I, [your name], commit to the following..."
Speak the words that feel most true.
You might say:
"I commit to honouring my energy, even when it's easier to push through."
"I choose to lead with compassion and make space for my intuition."
"I give myself permission to revise, rest, and return to alignment whenever I need."
"I trust myself to lead with heart."
This is your soul contract.
Not a pressure. Not a rule.
Just a remembering.

Calling in Angelic Support

Even the best architect knows they don't build alone. They have a team. They call in skilled support to help bring the blueprint to life.

It's the same for your soul. When you honour your soul contract, you don't have to carry it all by yourself.

Call on *Archangel Michael* to help you hold structure and strength. Imagine his deep cobalt-blue light surrounding your blueprint like protective scaffolding, keeping it safe as you build.

Call on *Archangel Gabriel* for clarity of vision. Picture Gabriel's golden-white light illuminating your plans, helping you see the next step with focus and confidence.

You are the architect, yes – but you are also supported. The unseen team is always with you, making sure the foundations you lay are protected, clear, and aligned with love.

Questions to Ponder and Journal

Take a moment to reflect:

If I were leading my Soul Company with full alignment... what would change?

_____
_____
_____
_____
_____

What would I stop doing?

_____
_____
_____
_____
_____

What would I start trusting?

_____

_____

_____

_____

What would I no longer carry just to keep the peace?

_____

_____

_____

_____

Let your answers be honest.
No fixing. Just noticing. That's where it begins.

Alisonism

"I have the power to hire what serves me – and fire what no longer does."

༄

Mantra for the Soul Architect

"I built this life on soul and love."

(As you say it, hum the tune of *We Built This City*. Let the rhythm anchor the words into your body. Feel the mantra not just in your mind, but flowing through your whole being.)

CHAPTER SEVEN

Sacred Stillness and Soothing
*(Regulating your nervous system
and integrating gently.)*

After all the building, aligning, hiring and firing… there comes a moment to pause.

To step back from the blueprint.

To feel what's been stirred.

To soothe what's still tender.

This is the chapter where we stop doing – and start being.

Because becoming isn't just about action.

It's about restoration. Regulation. Remembering what safety feels like inside your own body.

Stillness isn't the absence of movement – it's the presence of peace.

It's where the real integration happens.

It's where the nervous system catches up.

It's where the soul can finally exhale.

There's a healing power in stillness – and this chapter is devoted to it.

Why Self-Regulation Matters

Your nervous system is always working behind the scenes.

It's your body's internal wiring – constantly scanning for safety, connection, or threat.

When you're calm and connected, you're in what's called a regulated state.

This is when your body can digest, heal, think clearly, and rest.

But when you're stressed, overwhelmed, or emotionally flooded, your nervous system shifts into protection mode.

You might feel anxious, shut down, snappy, exhausted, or like you're 'buzzing' but can't slow down.

That's dysregulation – and it's more common than most people realise.

We all go in and out of these states. That's normal.

But the goal isn't to never get dysregulated – it's to know how to come back.

That's where self-regulation comes in.

Self-regulation means you know how to bring yourself back to centre – to soothe your system and return to a state of safety.

It's the difference between reacting from panic… and responding with presence.

This isn't about perfection.

It's about awareness.

It's about having tools that work for you – breathing, grounding, movement, sound, stillness – and using them gently, in real time.

The more we practise self-regulation, the more our system learns:

"I'm safe. I can handle this. I know how to come home to myself."

The Vagus Nerve: Your Calm Pathway

If your nervous system had a secret weapon… it would be the vagus nerve.

The vagus nerve is the longest cranial nerve in the body.

It runs from your brainstem, down through your throat, heart, lungs, and all the way into your digestive system.

It's like a communication superhighway between your brain and your body – especially your heart and gut.

When your vagus nerve is activated in a healthy way, it helps bring your body into a calm, relaxed state.

It slows your heart rate, deepens your breath, improves digestion, and signals to your system:

You're safe. You can rest.

This is called parasympathetic activation – the part of your nervous system responsible for rest, healing, and repair.

The science behind this is known as **Polyvagal Theory,** developed by *Dr Stephen Porges*. His research shows how our nervous system is constantly scanning for cues of safety or threat – and how simple practices like breath, sound, and grounding can help guide us back into balance.

But when you're constantly stressed or overstimulated, the vagus nerve isn't getting the signal it needs.

That's when anxiety, shutdown, tension, and emotional reactivity take over.

The good news?

There are simple ways to stimulate the vagus nerve and bring yourself back into balance.

- Gentle breathing
- Humming or chanting
- Splashing cold water on your face
- Singing

- Touching your heart space
- Slow movement and grounding

These are the practices we're about to explore – practical, powerful ways to help your system flick the internal switch from stress... to soothing.

Grounding: Coming Back to Earth

When your mind is racing or your emotions feel like too much, the first thing to come back to is your body.

And the easiest way to come back to your body... is through the Earth.

Grounding is the practice of reconnecting with your physical self and the world around you.

It's not a concept – it's an experience.

It reminds your nervous system: I'm here. I'm safe. I'm supported.

There's science behind this too.

Studies show that direct contact with the Earth – walking barefoot on grass, soil, or sand – can reduce inflammation, balance cortisol levels, improve sleep, and regulate mood.

It actually shifts the electrical activity in the body and supports a more balanced nervous system.

Grounding can also look like:

- Lying on the floor and feeling its weight beneath you
- Placing your hand on your heart or belly
- Pressing your feet into the ground and noticing the support
- Touching a tree or holding a grounding crystal
- Using your senses to name 5 things you see, 4 you touch, 3 you hear, 2 you smell, 1 you taste

These are quiet anchors.

They bring you out of spiralling thoughts and back into your body.

Back into now.

A Simple Grounding Practice

- **Pause and Notice**

Sit or stand comfortably.

Let your eyes soften or close.

Take one slow breath – in through the nose... out through the mouth.

- **Feel Your Feet**

Bring your attention down to your feet.

Feel them pressing into the ground.

Imagine roots growing from your soles into the Earth.

- **Anchor Into Your Body**

Gently place a hand on your heart or belly.

Let it remind your body: *"I'm here. I've got you."*

- **Engage Your Senses**

Notice:

- 5 things you can see
- 4 things you can touch
- 3 things you can hear
- 2 things you can smell
- 1 thing you can taste

- **Close With Intention**

Take one more breath.

Whisper to yourself: *"I am grounded. I am safe. I am here."*

The Healing Power of Sound

Sound is one of the simplest, most natural ways to calm the nervous system – and you don't need to sing or speak perfectly.

You just need to vibrate.

When you hum, chant, or use your voice with intention, it sends waves of vibration through your body.

These vibrations stimulate the vagus nerve and help shift you into calm.

In fact, I've been known to sing or chant in clinic, car and shower – sometimes quietly... and sometimes not so quietly!

Often, it flows out intuitively. I don't always know why in the moment – but the energy shifts, and that's what matters.

Sound-based practices I often use include:

- Humming
- Chanting simple sounds like *"Hum," "Om,"* or *"Ah"*
- Singing – in the car, in the shower, or during a session
- Toning long vowel sounds like *"Ooooo"* or *"Eeeee"*

The goal isn't performance – it's regulation.

Even 30 seconds of sound can flick the switch from tension to softness.

Author's Note: In clinic, I've often been known to hum or sing with clients, intuitively using sound as a sacred frequency for peace. Sometimes it's the simple hum of *"Hum,"* other times it's an 80s' song that flows out without me planning it. I've watched shoulders drop, eyes soften, and even bursts of laughter ripple through the room. The vibration does the work. Sound reaches places words can't – and often, it's this simplicity that brings the deepest calm.

Two Soothing Breath Practices

- **Box Breathing**

Great for anxious minds and overthinking.
- Inhale for 4 counts
- Hold for 4 counts
- Exhale for 4 counts
- Hold for 4 counts

Repeat for a few rounds.

Picture drawing a square with each breath. Remember to be gentle with yourself here.

- **Ocean Breath (Vagal Toning Breath)**

This is a favourite in clinic. Many of my clients connect with the ocean deeply – it's a place where we naturally let go for relaxation.

- Inhale through the nose for 4 counts (if you can)
- Exhale slowly through the mouth for 6–8 counts, making a soft *"Haaaa"* or wave-like sound in your throat

Repeat for several rounds.

This breath mimics the sound of waves and helps release stuck energy – gently massaging the vagus nerve and soothing the system.

Why the Beach Calms the Soul

I love the beach, and there's a reason the ocean makes us feel better – and it's backed by science.

- Waves create rhythmic sound that calms brain activity
- Negative ions in the air may boost serotonin and reduce inflammation
- The colour blue has been shown to lower heart rate and blood pressure
- Barefoot contact with sand supports grounding and electrical regulation in the body
- Salty air and natural scents soothe the limbic system – the part of the brain that governs emotion

The beach actually regulates us.

And if you can't be there physically, you can still bring its essence into your body and breath.

Even something as simple as looking at a beach scene on your phone, while breathing gently, can begin to shift your nervous system.

Let the image soften your body. Let the rhythm of the waves settle your breath. Let your system remember what peace feels like.

A Simple Beach Visualisation

Get comfortable.
Place a hand on your heart or belly.
Close your eyes.
Breathe in... and out... like a wave.
Now imagine you're standing at the edge of the ocean.
Feel the warm sand under your feet.
Waves gently roll in and out.
Breathe with their rhythm.
Now begin a slow walk along the shoreline.
Each step, the water washes over your feet.
Let it carry away stress, tension, and anything you no longer need.
You are supported.
You are steady.
You are being cleansed.
When ready, breathe in deeply...
Exhale with a soft sigh...
Open your eyes and return, bringing the ocean's calm with you.

Faith: The Unseen Anchor

In moments of stillness, many people feel something greater.
A whisper of reassurance.
A feeling of being held.
A knowing beyond logic.
Call it God.
Call it Source.
Call it your angels, guides, or simply the Universe.
There's no right or wrong way to name this presence – only the invitation to trust it.
Having faith means allowing something bigger than your mind to guide you.
It's not about bypassing reality or outsourcing responsibility – it's about opening to unseen support.
It's what carries us through the unknown.
It's the breath in the darkness.
It's the nudge on the path.
It's the reminder: You are never alone.
Let your stillness be a space where faith can rise again.

Angelic Soothing

In stillness, you may also sense the quiet presence of your angelic team.

Archangel Raphael often draws near in these moments, surrounding you in waves of soft emerald light that gently steadies and renews you.

Mother Mary may appear as a soft blue shawl gently resting on your shoulders, reminding you that you are safe, cherished, and allowed to rest.

You don't need a formal prayer to welcome them. A simple whisper, *"Be with me,"* is enough – and peace will begin to rise within you.

℮

The Power of Doing Less

We live in a world where busyness is the norm, worn like a badge of honour – and rest is often mistaken for laziness.

But doing less isn't giving up.

It's making space.

For your nervous system to settle.

For your soul to speak.

For creativity and clarity to rise from the quiet.

When you slow down, your body stops running on survival – and begins to trust again.

Give yourself permission to pause.

Stillness is not a failure.

It's wisdom.

It's medicine.

It's where the real becoming begins.

Questions to Ponder and Journal

Where in my life am I being called to pause?

What part of me softens when I give myself permission to rest?

Where can I make space for stillness in my week?

Alisonism

"Doing less creates space for more of me. I give myself permission to pause."

⁓

Mantra for Stillness

"In stillness, I remember I am safe. In stillness, I remember I am whole."

CHAPTER EIGHT

Becoming You – Stepping Into What's Next
(Anchors for the road ahead.)

Hey, by the way – a little heads up. This next chapter is jam-packed with soul-filled tools, metaphors, and practices. Don't feel you need to scoop them all up at once. Just notice which one makes your shoulders drop, or your breath soften, and start there. The rest will be waiting for you when you're ready.

Alisonism

"My past does not dictate my future."

The Weight of Yesterday

We all carry echoes of the past. Sometimes they're loud – heartbreak, betrayal, disappointment. Sometimes they're quiet – a strange unease that doesn't seem to belong to this life.

In clinic, I see fears tied to many layers:

• **This lifetime** – fear of being alone, fear of men, fear of being unsafe.

• **Ancestral patterns** – fear of being born female, fear of speaking truth.

• **Soul memories** – fear of punishment for standing tall or being who you really are.

Fear often links to control. Gripping the steering wheel too tightly. Trying to manage outcomes, keeping everyone else happy, or staying safe by staying small.

And yet, here's the truth: Having fear means you care – it shows your heart is awake.

Looking Fear in the Eye

Kyle Gray, in **Warrior of Light,** teaches that when you look fear in the eye, it loses its power. This is one of my all-time favourite books and one of the most used in my clinic. Its wisdom shows up again and again when I'm guiding clients through their fears.

So when fear rises, instead of pushing it away, meet it directly. Whisper:

"Fear, I see you. I see you for what you are."

By naming it, you shrink it. What once felt like a shadow chasing you is revealed as a pattern – not truth.

These old imprints often sound like this:

"If I suffer, I'm safe. It's familiar. It's all I know. If I stay small, I stay safe."

"If I speak up, I'll be punished. If I show who I really am, I'll be cast out."

"Don't shine too brightly. Don't draw attention. It's dangerous."

These whispers may feel stitched into your very bones, but they are not who you are. They are survival strategies that once served – but no longer fit.

Forgiveness as Freedom

The way forward is forgiveness.

Forgiving yourself for what you didn't know. For what was out of your control. For how you coped when you were simply trying to get through.

We don't know what we don't know. And when forgiveness lands, the past loosens its grip.

A Declaration of Release

Here is my own take on *Kyle Gray's* **Persecution Prayer** – rewritten for this journey of Becoming:

Declaration
Dear Universe,
I am not here to suffer in this lifetime.
There has been too much suffering in my past.
I now release all ties, fears, and experiences with suffering – in this life and in my past lifetimes – and I reclaim my power.
I now declare I am unbound and free to be me.
I fill my heart and every cell in my body with love, light, empowerment, and freedom.

Alisonism

"I am unbound and free to be me."

Outdated Software and Default Settings

Old fears and patterns are like outdated software running quietly in the background. They slow us down, glitch our progress, and sometimes override the new programs we're trying to run.

The good news? You can hit delete. You can drag old files – those beliefs that no longer serve – into the bin. You can update your system.

But here's the key question: Do you give yourself permission to accept the software update?

Because no matter how many upgrades are available, nothing changes until you click yes.

And sometimes, even after an update, we still default back to the old wiring. Not because we've failed – but because the system is familiar with that pathway. When you're tired, stressed, or triggered, you might momentarily return to default.

That's okay. It doesn't undo your progress. It simply shows you where the old coding still lives – and gives you another chance to choose differently.

Every time you cancel-clear-delete, flip the script, and heart-connect, you're teaching your system a new command. You're rewriting the code.

Sometimes, though, those old files don't just slow you down – they keep popping up like windows you never asked to open. A memory, a thought loop, an old 'what if' running on repeat.

When that happens, try treating it like a folder on your laptop. You don't need to delete it – because it did happen, and it shaped you – but you also don't need it running in front of you every day. So you drag it into Archive.

It's still stored in your library, safe and acknowledged, but no longer demanding constant attention. You get to choose what stays open on your screen – and what gets filed away.

This isn't denial. It's discernment – the art of clear, wise choosing. Not reacting out of habit or fear, but pausing long enough to sense: Is this mine? Does this serve me? Do I keep this open, or do I file it away?

That inner filter helps you decide what deserves your energy and what doesn't.

I actually used this myself the other night. I couldn't sleep because memories of my teenage years kept looping, like a broken record (I know, can you believe it!!). Eventually I remembered my own strategy – and imagined myself dragging those files into the Archive. Straight away, my mind quietened and I drifted off. It worked like a charm.

A Gentle Practice: Archiving the Loop

And if you want to try this yourself, here's a simple way to do it:

1. Notice the pop-up.

When a memory or thought keeps looping, acknowledge it. *"Ah, here's that file again."*

2. Pause and choose.

Ask yourself: *"Is this serving me right now? Do I need it open on my screen, or can it be stored away?"*

3. Drag it to Archive.

Imagine physically moving the thought into a folder called Archive on your inner desktop. Know it's stored safely, but you don't have to keep staring at it.

4. Close the window.

Visualise clicking the little 'x'. Take a soft breath out as you do – that exhale is your reset.

5. Return to the present.

Place your hand on your heart and whisper:

"That was then. This is now. I am free to be me."

Use it anytime your mind starts recycling old stories. Over time, your system learns: Not every file deserves to stay open.

A Gentle Practice: The Flame of Freedom

1. Sit in stillness. Place your hand on your heart.

2. Imagine a candle flame glowing inside your chest – warm, steady, unwavering.

3. With each breath, let it expand into every cell.

4. Whisper softly:

"I am not bound by my past."

"I forgive what I could not control."

"I am free to be me."

5. Stay until you feel spaciousness – as if invisible cords have loosened around you.

The Soul Permission Slip of Acceptance

You no longer need to wait for permission from the world. Healing and becoming are about meeting yourself exactly where you are – and giving yourself full permission to do so.

Write yourself a soul-filled permission slip. It might sound like this:

"I give myself permission to rest."

"I give myself permission to speak with clarity."

"I give myself permission to thrive without guilt."

"I completely accept who I am in this moment without judgment."

When you speak these words, something shifts. You drop out of striving. You stop measuring yourself against who you were yesterday or who you think you should be tomorrow. You soften into now.

Acceptance doesn't mean you'll never change. It means you recognise your worth in this very breath. It creates space for peace to rise.

So sign it. Date it. Carry it close. Let it remind you: You are the one writing the rules now – and the first rule is that you are already enough.

Future Visioning: Where to From Here?

This book has been a roadmap to a peaceful soul. But a roadmap isn't the destination. The real question now is: Where do you want to go?

You've travelled through the teachings, practised the tools, and peeled back the layers. You've released, remembered, and reclaimed. Now you stand at the threshold – healing has given you the keys, and only you can decide where to drive next.

- Imagine your future self – free from fear. How do you walk into a room? How do you speak? What kind of mornings do you gift yourself?
- Picture your 'soul car' from Chapter 3 – but now upgraded. Where do you want to drive next? What scenery calls your name?

You don't need the full map today. All you need is a sense of direction, a felt vision that lights your body from the inside out. The rest will unfold as you go.

This is your invitation to dream forward – to create with choice, with clarity, and with soul.

Peaceful Soul Toolkit

A few simple anchors to carry forward:

- **Daily grounding:** Two minutes of feet-to-floor, hand-to-heart breathing.
- **Mantra:** *"I am unbound. I am Becoming."*
- **Reset ritual:** Cancel. Clear. Delete. Then Flip the Script. And always heart-connect.
- **Soul check-in:** Ask, *"Am I steering with trust or with fear?"*
- **Archive reset:** When an old memory pops up, drag it to archive and breathe, *"That was then, this is now."*

These aren't chores – they're reminders.

Questions to Ponder and Journal

What fears feel like they don't fully belong to this life?

Where in my life am I gripping the steering wheel too tightly?

If I forgave myself for not knowing what I didn't know, what would shift?

What vision do I hold for my life when fear no longer writes the script?

_____
_____
_____
_____
_____

What permission do I most need to give myself right now?

_____
_____
_____
_____
_____

How does it feel in my body to affirm: *"I completely accept who I am in this moment without judgment?"*

_____
_____
_____
_____
_____

CHAPTER NINE

Poetry in Motion
(Heartfelt encouragement for the readers' ongoing journey.)

Healing doesn't unfold in a straight line – it moves like the ocean. There are ebbs and flows.

Moments where you rise with clarity.

Moments where you pull inward and need to rest.

Like the breath.

Like the tide.

Like becoming.

This chapter isn't about rushing forward.

It's about recognising that you're already in motion – even when you're still.

Even when you're simply keeping your head above water.

There's nothing wrong with pausing in the shallows.

And there's nothing wrong with riding the wave when the momentum returns.

You don't have to fight the current.

You can ride it.

As my clients know, I often say, *"We're like onions."*

We're layered – emotionally, energetically, generationally.

Healing doesn't happen all at once.

It peels back, layer by layer, breath by breath, until we return to something softer.

Something true.

Becoming You is Poetry in Motion

You're not a fixed point on a map.
You're a living poem – unfolding line by line, moment by moment.
Some days, your rhythm will feel strong and steady.
Other days, it might stammer, scatter, or go quiet.
But even in the silence… you're still becoming.

Healing is like poetry – it doesn't need to rhyme, and it doesn't always make sense in the beginning. Some lines arrive raw and jagged, others soft and lyrical. But over time, the rhythm emerges. The pieces connect. And the whole becomes something greater than each line on its own.

Poetry isn't polished on the first draft – and neither are we.
We revise.
We rework.
We soften and edit and underline what matters.
You don't need to have the perfect words.
You just need to stay in the process.
Let life move through you. Let it shape you. Let it speak.
This is what Poetry in Motion really means:
You are the verse.
You are the breath.
You are the one who gets to choose how the next line is written.
Not perfectly.
But with presence.
And with heart.

The Moment It All Began for Me: (my poetry)

I didn't set out to write this book.

There was no plan. No outline. No perfect time.

It started with a quiet Sunday afternoon – just me, lying on the couch, not trying to channel or create.

I was simply being.

And then… something opened.

Words began to rise – not from my mind, but from somewhere deeper.

They spilled in without warning.

Verses I didn't fully understand, but recognised in my body.

Ancient-feeling. Familiar. True.

It was a whisper from my soul – one I'd been too busy to hear until I slowed down enough to listen.

Those first few lines became the seed of this book.

A remembering. A reckoning. A return.

I still don't know if I wrote them… or if they wrote me.

Alison's Soul Script

(Transmission received in sacred stillness)

A soul script
Loveliness awakens like a gardenia
Threads of wonderment weave themselves through your being
You have become the heavenly Goddess
A cathedral to human spirit and a saviour to mere mortal
Love abides
Be still these sacred waters
Amen

– Alison Dunlop

Your Soul Promise

You don't need a five-year plan.

You don't need to have it all figured out.

But you can make a promise – from your soul, to yourself.

A promise to be gentle when things feel hard.

To stay open when you're tempted to shut down.

To honour your needs, your healing, and your wholeness – even when no one else sees it.

To hang in there when the waves feel big.

To rest when you need to.

To rise when you're ready.

And most of all... to live in a way that feels true to you.

This is your soul promise.

You don't need permission.

Just presence.

And a willingness to return – again and again – to the truth of who you are.

Take a moment to write your own Soul Promise. It doesn't need to be long – even one line is enough.

Ask yourself, *"What truth do I want to whisper to myself when things feel hard?"*

Let it be your own poem – a touchstone to return to when you forget.

Example:

"Dear Me,

"I promise to pause before I push.

"I promise to speak gently to myself.

"I promise to remember that I am already enough."

A Closing Ritual: Sealing the Becoming

Find a quiet moment.

You don't need candles or music – just your breath, your presence, and your willingness to meet yourself.

Place one hand on your heart, and one on your belly.

Feel the warmth of your own touch.

This body has carried you through every page.

This breath has been with you since the beginning.

Take a slow inhale.

And as you exhale, let go of any striving.

You don't need to become anything more right now.

You are here.

You are enough.

You are in motion – and you are whole.

Whisper this to yourself (or speak it aloud):

"I honour where I've been."

"I welcome where I'm going."

And I choose to meet myself, right here, in this moment – with kindness, truth, and grace.

If it feels right, invite a presence to witness this moment with you. An angel, a guide, an ancestor, or simply the presence of Love itself. Imagine them standing beside you, hand on your shoulder, affirming: *"You are safe. You are seen. You are Becoming."*

Take one more breath.

Let it feel like a soft exhale – a return.

You're already Becoming You.

Alisonism

"Even in stillness, you're still in motion."

☙

Mantra for Motion

"I flow with life. I am enough."

CLOSING WORDS

A Love Note to the Becoming One

I write this love note, hand on heart –
because you've made it here.
Not just to the final pages,
but through your own becoming.

This isn't an ending.
It's a soft beginning.
You've peeled back layers.
You've remembered your essence.
You've touched truth, tenderness, and trust.

And even if there were pauses…
Even if you skipped pages, cried in the middle, or doubted along the way –
you stayed.
You chose to meet yourself.
And that matters more than words can say.

Beloved one,
brave tender soul –
together we have conquered doubt,
met the ego, and learned to ride the tide.

Go forth with renewed vigour and shine.
Let your soul be a beacon of presence.
And may your lightness carry you confidently on the waves of life.

With blessings,
Alison

༄

Alisonism

"Home is where the heart is – and the soul knows the way."

BONUS CHAPTER

Becoming One – Alisonisms from the Healing Room
A cheeky companion for the curious Becoming One

I f only the walls of my healing room could talk...
They'd whisper about the quiet breakthroughs, the deep exhales, and the sacred stillness.

And then they'd giggle – because let's be honest, they've also heard me laugh a little too loudly at my own quirks and metaphors.

Over the years, I've come up with so many soul metaphors, odd-but-accurate comparisons, and cheeky truths that just... work. They stick in your memory, soothe the nervous system, and help translate the unseeable into something tangible.

This final bonus chapter is a gentle nod to the practical magic that gets sprinkled in between the big energetic shifts.

It's sort of like an Alison blooper reel.

1. Flick the Shit

This one's a classic Alisonism. If I had a dollar for every time I've said it in clinic, I'd be retired on a beach with a cocktail.

"*Flick the shit*" is my signature shorthand for releasing the energy that's not yours to carry.

Because let's be real – we're all energetic sponges sometimes.

Clients, colleagues, family, random people in the supermarket... their stuff can stick.

Suddenly, you're carrying tension, sadness, anger, or a general sense of heaviness – and it's not even yours.

So what do we do?

We flick it. Literally.

Sometimes I even catch myself doing it mid-conversation with someone down the street – hands behind my back, fingers flicking away discreetly.

It's not just a cheeky move.

It's a signal to the body and energy field:

This doesn't belong to me. I don't have to keep it. I choose to let it go.

You can do it too – anytime, anywhere.

Energetic hygiene doesn't have to be fancy. It just needs awareness and a flicking strategy.

Try this:

Take a moment to breathe, tune in to your body, and ask:

"*Is this mine to hold?*"

If the answer is no – flick it away with intention.

Flick it off your arms, your chest, your shoulders.

Release it like you mean it.

2. Bubble Up

"Bubble up" is a phrase I use often when a client needs a cocoon – a protective energetic shield between themselves and the noise of the world.

It's not about hiding or disconnecting.

It's about honouring your energetic space.

It's about staying present in your own body, in your own field, without being overwhelmed by other people's stuff.

Some days we're sensitive. Some days we've already given too much.

Bubble up gives you permission to draw that line energetically.

I always do this one before venturing to the supermarket.

Try this:

Close your eyes and take a few soft breaths.

Now imagine a light-filled bubble gently expanding around you.

You get to choose the colour, texture, and feel.

It might be glittery, transparent, silky, or dense like fog.

This is your bubble – a sacred space for you to rest and reset.

Repeat this daily if you have to, especially after Flicking the Shit!

3. Flip the Script

You know those sneaky thoughts that slip in without warning?

The ones that whisper:

"You're not good enough."

"Who do you think you are?"

"It's too late now."

Yeah. Those.

Flip the Script is how we stop them in their tracks and choose a better internal dialogue.

It's about gently catching the thought – and choosing to rewire it.

Not with forced positivity, but with truth.

With choice.

Instead of:

"I always mess this up."

Try:

"I'm learning, and I give myself grace."

Try this – when a thought feels heavy or self-critical, whisper:

"Hang on. Let's flip the script."

Then speak a new one.

One that's kind, honest, and empowering.

Repeat it out loud or in your mind until your nervous system believes it's safe to trust this new truth.

4. Cancel. Clear. Delete.

This one works like an energetic backspace key.

When you catch yourself (or someone else) saying something unkind, limiting, or just plain unhelpful – say:

"Cancel. Clear. Delete."

It's not about judgment.

It's about energetic housekeeping.

Words carry vibration. And what we speak – we energise.

So when the gossip starts, when the self-criticism rolls in, or when you say something you don't want to feed… clear it.

Try this:

You don't need a ritual. Just awareness.

Say it softly or in your mind:

"Cancel. Clear. Delete."

Then pause. Breathe. And speak something more aligned instead – and Flip the Script.

5. Archangel Michael, Whoosh Me

This one might make you laugh, but trust me – it works. One of my favourite phrases is:

"Archangel Michael, whoosh me."

After every client session I say it – often with a hand movement sweeping upwards – and I feel Michael's energy clear through me like a giant vacuum, lifting away anything I may have picked up. I trust him to transmute it all into love.

No, I'm not being weird when I say this. I know it might sound it sometimes, but it's one of those Alisonisms that stuck because it really does the job.

And you don't have to be a practitioner to use it. You can ask *Archangel Michael* to 'whoosh' you anytime:

- After a day at work.
- After shopping or being in crowded places.
- After socialising if you feel drained or heavy.

Try this:

- Stand or sit comfortably. Place your hand in front of you, ready to sweep upwards through your energy field – as if sending any heaviness straight up into the Heavens.
- Close your eyes and take a slow, steady breath.
- Say out loud (or silently in your mind):

"Archangel Michael, whoosh me."

- As you say it, sweep your hand upwards through your aura, guiding any energy that isn't yours to be lifted away.
- Imagine Michael's great light vacuuming up what no longer belongs to you and transmuting it into pure love.
- Take another breath and notice how you feel – lighter, clearer, more you.

Repeat whenever you need it. Quick, cheeky, and surprisingly powerful.

6. Beam Me Up, Scotty

Yes, this one comes straight from Star Trek. And yes, I'm a diehard Star Trek fan.

I often say this with clients as a strategy when life feels messy or overwhelming. It's my Alisonism shorthand for: *"Give me strength. Lift me above this situation so I can see it clearly."*

When you say, *"Beam me up, Scotty,"* you're choosing to rise above the density. Instead of being stuck in the tangle of emotion, you shift your perspective – looking at the situation from above, with more calmness, divine support, and intuitive guidance.

Try this:

• The next time you're caught in the middle of stress, pause and say, *"Beam me up, Scotty."*

• Imagine being lifted into a higher vantage point – as if you're hovering above the scene.

• From here, notice how the noise softens and you can see the bigger picture.

• Allow calm to land. Trust the guidance that comes when you view things from above.

It's cheeky, but it works. A reminder that you don't have to stay lost in space – you can always rise up, shift your perspective, and reconnect with clarity.

7. Shake It Off

Yes, I'm totally borrowing this one from Taylor Swift. *"Haters gonna hate, hate, hate, hate, hate…"* – you know the rest.

Sometimes life delivers comments, judgments, or energy that could stick if we let it. But here's the truth: What other people say usually says more about them than it does about you. You don't need to take it on. You don't need to carry it.

That's where Shake It Off comes in. It's my Alisonism for letting things roll off you like water off a duck's back.

And yes, in clinic my clients and I actually sing it – complete with big, silly hand actions. Because the fastest way to shift heaviness is to move your body, laugh, and refuse to let someone else's stuff define you.

Try this:

- The next time someone's words sting, crank up your inner (or actual) Taylor Swift.
- Say it, sing it, and move it out: *"Shake it off, shake it off!"*
- Do the hand flicks, the shoulder shimmies, the full-body shake if you dare.
- Sing at the top of your lungs. Get silly. Feel the weight fall away.

Not only will your nervous system thank you, but you'll remember that joy is a powerful cleanser too.

8. WIP – Work in Progress

This one still makes me smile. A client once told me she was a WIP. I looked at her blankly and asked, *"What's WIP?"* She roared laughing and said, *"Work in Progress."*

Being a work in progress actually takes the stress off Becoming. You don't have to arrive all at once. You don't need to perfect it, polish it, or prove it. You're allowed to be unfolding, learning, shifting. In fact, that's the whole point of this journey.

And here's the cheeky bit: Being a WIP makes you your own kind of VIP. You're important because you're growing and evolving.

Try this:

- The next time you're being hard on yourself, sing it out loud to the tune of the Jackson 5's ABC: *"W-I-P… it's easy as 1-2-3!"*
- Add a little shoulder shimmy or dance move if you dare.
- Let your body remember: You don't have to have it all sorted out to be fabulous!

Closing Note

These Alisonisms are not rules, they're reminders. They're the phrases, images, and shortcuts that help me (and my clients) shift out of fear and back into freedom.

Use the ones that land. Laugh at the cheeky ones. Share them with a friend who needs them. Most of all, let them remind you that healing doesn't have to be heavy – it can be light, simple, and even a little playful.

ACKNOWLEDGEMENTS

To my beautiful clients – thank you for trusting me with your hearts, your stories, your healing.

You have been my greatest teachers.

Every session, every tear, every spark of remembering has helped shape this work.

This book was born in those sacred moments. I hold deep gratitude for each of you.

To the quiet voice within – thank you for waiting patiently while I found my way back.

And to the mentor who first suggested – to my shock – that I write a book… thank you, Ross, for planting the seed I didn't know was ready to grow.

This book is for all who *'Are Becoming.'*

NOTES AND REFERENCES

If you'd like to explore some of the ideas in this book further, here are a few places to begin. These works have informed, inspired, and supported the practices shared in Becoming You.

Chapter 5:
The Heart and Coherence

• The research from the **HeartMath Institute** shows how the heart communicates with the brain, generates an electromagnetic field, and influences both our emotions and those around us. Their work also highlights the benefits of 'heart coherence' – calm, steady rhythms that support clarity, healing, and emotional balance.

Chapter 7:
The Nervous System and Safety

• *Stephen Porges*, through his **Polyvagal Theory,** explains how our nervous system constantly scans for safety or threat, shaping how we feel and respond in daily life. His work helps us understand why practices like breath, sound, and gentle regulation bring us back to calm.

Grounding and Connection with the Earth

• Research on **Earthing** or **Grounding** has shown that direct contact with the Earth (like walking barefoot on grass, soil, or sand) can reduce inflammation, balance cortisol, and improve mood and sleep.

The Ocean's Calming Power

• Studies on natural environments – especially the ocean – show how rhythmic wave sounds, salty air, negative ions, and the colour blue all help regulate the nervous system and restore emotional balance.

Continue Your Journey

If this book has spoken to your soul and you'd like to go deeper into releasing limiting beliefs and reconnecting with your true self, I invite you to explore my **Limitless Recode Mini Course.**

It's a gentle yet powerful 8-module journey designed to help you shift old patterns, rewire your inner dialogue, and step into greater freedom and confidence — at your own pace.

Check it out here: *Limitless Recode Mini Course* by *Alison Dunlop*
https://alisondunlopkinesiology.com.au/limitless-recode-mini-course/

RECOMMENDED READING AND INSPIRATIONS

The following teachers and texts have shaped my own journey. They may also offer wisdom, comfort, or inspiration as you continue yours.

Kyle Gray

Kyle's books and oracle decks make working with angels feel accessible and modern. His grounded approach weaves the mystical into everyday life in a way that is both gentle and empowering.

Radleigh Valentine

Radleigh brings a playful yet profound energy to his teachings on angel wisdom and intuitive living. His work often reminds us that guidance can be joyful, light-hearted, and still deeply transformative.

Dougall Fraser

Dougall offers soulful insights into healing, energy, and the deeper patterns that shape our lives. His work has helped me deepen my understanding of how spirit and human experience weave together.

John Edward

John is a pioneer in the field of mediumship, known for his ability to bridge the seen and unseen with clarity and compassion. His work affirms that love and connection continue beyond this life.

These aren't required readings, but invitations. If you feel drawn, explore them – and notice what resonates with your own soul.

The Ascentian Prayer
by Alison Dunlop

Thank you, Universe and Angels,
for nurturing and supporting my mind, body, and soul.
I trust that I am always Divinely guided and lovingly protected.
I listen to my intuition and know I am safe and secure surrounded
by Universal love.

I am one, I am Love.
And so it is.

NOTES

NOTES

NOTES

NOTES

www.ingramcontent.com/pod-product-compliance
Lightning Source LLC
Chambersburg PA
CBHW061729070526
44583CB00024B/3067